Bobbi,

Enjoy, babe! Can't
to hear what you think. ...
you for being an inspiration.

xx,
Sydney

BARNEYS,

BERGDORFS

&

BILL$

Sydney Hedberg

Library of Congress Cataloging-in-Publication Data

Hedberg, Sydney
    Barneys, Bergdorfs & Bill$: A gGrlfriend's Guide to Finance
/ Hedberg, Sydney.
        p. cm.

    ISBN 978-1-48356-188-2

    1. Young women – Finance, Personal. 2. Young women –
Life skills guides. 3. Adulthood – Transition. I. Title.

First published in October 2015.
Revised and reprinted in January 2016.

Printed in the United States of America by BookBaby.

Dedicated to the all of the girls
determined to rise and change the world.

*"Barneys, Bergdorfs & Bill$ eloquently breaks down
the barriers of tedious financial topics and turns them
into a fabulous conversation that all young female
professionals can easily follow. This Girlfriends Guide
to Finance is a must-read for all girls who are
determined to take on the world in their Loubs"*
–Lauren P.

*"I love the comments about what we spend our money
on and how relatable it is. The examples are so helpful
at helping me learn how to budget"* – **Fitzhugh B.**

*"I wish I had this book while I was still in school
because it could have saved me from making a LOT of
financial mistakes. I love how it isn't full of fluff but
gets right down to the point so it's easy to understand"*
– **Mary Katherine B.**

CONTENTS

HAVE NO FEAR

Investopedia defines "financial literacy" as "the ability to understand how money works in the world. How someone earns or makes it, how that person manages it, invests it (turns it into more) and donates it to help others."

When I bring up any type of financial topic with the majority of my friends, their interest is lost within the blink of an eye. Just because I find it interesting doesn't mean my friends feel the same way. Some would probably equate my rambling to watching paint dry. Are the topics of money management, investments and the stock market riveting stuff to everyone? No. Is it imperative that everyone know a least a LITTLE about it...YOU BETCHA! I am here to help make finance more understandable and relevant to your life.

Financial literacy is a serious issue in the United States – especially for us, ladies. Many women select majors that do not place an emphasis on the importance of knowing financial topics. This means fewer of us are learning the basics of accounting, economics and simple money management skills. I am not a feminist by any means, but here are some stats from *Women, Money and Success Magazine*:

• Women earn 25% less money than men.

• Women save less money (blame it on Barneys and Bergdorf Goodman) leaving them less confident about their financial abilities and more reliant on men.

• 50% of marriages end in divorce (getting that MRS degree isn't the answer), after which the woman's quality of life often drops substantially because she has not been the one managing the household money.

There is, however, also good evidence to suggest that women exercise greater and greater financial self-determination. Women actually save more, as a percentage of their incomes, than men do, but the average balance in a man's 401(k) is about 50% greater because men still outearn women (Tara Siegel Bernard, "Financial Advice for Women, From Women," *New York Times*, 11/7/15, B5).

Despite this gender-gap when it comes to income, the Pew Research Center has shown that "Women are now the primary breadwinners in 40 percent of all households with children under 18," while "the proportion of married mothers out-earning their husbands has also risen, from 4 percent in 1960 to 17 percent in 2015" (Richard V. Reeves and Isabel V.

Sawhill, "Men's Lib!" *New York Times*, 11/15/15, SR6). So we are on the rise, ladies!

In light of this, my main goals are to make young women feel more confident by expanding their financial knowledge; to help these women grasp, or at least be familiar with, basic financial concepts and how money works; to suggest how to make your money grow with smart investments; and to emphasize the importance of balancing your budget and to offer advice to help you do so.

I am attempting to break down tricky financial concepts into simple, straightforward, and easy to learn topics. There are other guides to finance out there, but they weren't written by people our age who relate to what our lives are like right now. Being young means living it up. I love to take trips with my girlfriends, eat at fancy and expensive places, and live life luxuriously…but that will not be your reality forever unless you take a step back and keep tabs on your finances.

Knowledge makes you confident, powerful and a force to be reckoned with – those are 3 traits I know we all want to add to our résumés.

GIRLFRIEND'S GUIDE

Before beginning this book I *highly* recommend you keep a notebook handy to jot down little notes. You will need one in the last section to layout all of your finances!

Before beginning this journey, I polled a few of my Tri Delta sisters to see if they would have an interest in learning more about budgeting and their finances. Overwhelmingly their answers were a resounding *YES*.

With most of them having graduated recently from Ole Miss, lots are hearing the phrase every child fears: "cut off." Prepare to drive your Mercedes into the harsh reality of the "real world."

My Greek sisters' monetary responsibilities now include:
- Rent
- Food
- Clothes
- Gas
- Car insurance
- Utilities
- Cell phone
- Travel – or any other type of leisure

College is easy for some and very difficult for others. Some float by debt free with their parents or guardians paying their immense tuition costs. On the other hand, many students are inundated with the burden of student loans they will eventually have to pay back with the help of their hard-earned paychecks. Say goodbye to your shoe fetish and hello to interest payments and taxes.

When I asked my friends about their knowledge of finance, most said it ended with the notion not to spend more than you have in your bank account...which essentially is the big picture. However, it's inevitable that you will one day be facing your budget all by your lonesome, so there are numerous specific topics we all need to be familiar with.

Life is expensive. Seriously. I had a wake up to this the other day. My dad called me before I went to my internship and happened to mention the credit card bill. I have two cards: one with my name on it but which is paid by my parents, and a debit card that is my PERSONAL money. On my parents' card I put gas, food and miscellaneous things such as car maintenance. Shopping, travel – anything else that I choose to do – I pay for from my own account.

So how much did I spend on my parents' card in a month? $1,500. Whoops!

That incited me to do a little digging into my personal Wells Fargo account. In the past 18 months I have deposited $31,710. I currently have $3,578. That means in the past 18 months I have spent $28,132. My jaw dropped.

Where in the hell did all of that money go? I'll tell you where it went. It was the trip to NYC. It was the five-star spa and hotel I vacationed at in Nassau. The pair of spring collection Gucci shoes I HAD to have from Bergdorf Goodman. It was the tri-weekly trips to Starbucks. And then just like that, 28 grand out the window.

While I consider myself very financially responsible, I am all about living big. I like the finer things in life and I don't apologize for that. I have worked hard in school because I know the lifestyle I desire isn't going to pay for itself. With all of that being said, I am ALL about a deal! Priceline is my best friend. The sale rack at Neiman Marcus is the first thing I spot. If I'm getting a deal it totally justifies me buying it...right?

Sometimes it's dangerous to reason with yourself: "with a sale like that I can't afford *not* to buy it."

Taking a serious look at my bank account is making me rethink all of this, and that has prompted this book's plan to show my fellow girls – who are one day going to rule the world – to do the same.

As women we are not at a disadvantage to men. Sometimes we may be conditioned to think we are, and fall into saying "I think I'll finish college, get married, work for two years, have a baby, and then my husband will earn a paycheck for both of us and I will stay home"...(not to diminish how difficult the job of raising babies is!)

To each her own, but whether you want to be the next Sheryl Sandberg (like myself), or want to be the loving stay-at-home-mom – or both...go girl! – this information is important for everyone because you never know what funny curveballs life is going to throw at you.

TOPIC #1: CHECKING AND SAVINGS

We will begin with the basics: checking and savings accounts. When you take money to your bank it generally goes to one of two places: your checking account (typically also tied to a debit card) or savings account. Here is the difference between them.

Checking Account. This account is for daily transactions or ongoing monthly expenses: trips to the grocery store, shopping, rent, etc.

Savings Account. This is a place to put money for future use: an emergency fund, large purchases, or maybe investments.

Most people, especially us in college, deposit ready cash to our checking accounts because we want the money NOW. However, by doing this we are giving up a HUGE opportunity to do something else with that money. That opportunity comes in the form of an "interest rate."

The money you deposit in these accounts is SAFE. Think back to Great Depression when people needed spendable cash desperately, but found their banks wiped out. Another

5

example would be the recent desperation in Greece, where everyone was limited to daily withdrawals of only €60 to prevent "bank runs."

This is no longer an issue because every deposit you make today (up to a total of $250,000 per account) is backed by the government's **Federal Deposit Insurance Corporation** (FDIC) established in 1933. This means is your money is safe.

If you have a debit card you can set up a monthly transfer of money from your checking account to your savings. This eliminates the thought process behind actually placing money in your debit savings account. It is automatically transferred and will now sit in your savings account earning a very low interest rate but an interest rate nonetheless.

Many don't see the point of letting their money sit in an account when it earns .02%, but, hey, it's better than letting it sit in your checking earning 0%!

TOPIC #2: INTEREST RATES & THE FED

Interest rates are determined by numerous factors and are set by the Federal Reserve. The **Federal Reserve**, also known as the "Fed," regulates the U.S. monetary policy and the nation's financial system. The Fed exists to ensure the financial stability of the U.S. Their success or failure is felt worldwide and on Main and Wall Streets. When your money sits in a checking account it earns no interest because that cash is readily accessible to you. In order to make interest on your money you must be "giving" it up for a period of time.

With a savings account, your balance grows over time not only with each deposit, but also increases thanks to **compound interest.** This is how compound interest works:

You deposit $2,000 in your savings account; this is known as your **principal**. If the annual interest rate is 5% this means that after twelve months you will have made $100 in interest. Simple as that...all you had to do was let your money sit there and grow. The next year you will be earning 5% again, but instead of accruing only on your initial $2,000 principal it will now grow on the full $2,100 in your savings account and you will earn $105 in interest the second year. Here is a chart to show how much patience can pay off. *Note this is not always how interest will work because most interest rates "fluctuate" (go up and down). An interest rate of 5% is also EXTREMELY high and unrealistic.

Years	Interest Earned on Principal	Total Interest Earned	Balance
1	$100	$100	$2,100
2	$105	$205	$2,205
3	$110.25	$315.25	$2,315
4	$115.76	$431.01	$2,431.01
5	$121.55	$552.56	$2,552.56
10	$155.13	$1,257.79	$3,257.79
20	$252.70	$3,306.60	$5,306.60
30	$411.61	$6,643.88	$8,643.88

As you can see, each year your interest amount is increasing more and more. After 30 years, you will more than quadruple your initial $2,000 investment. Now 30 years seems like a long time, but you had to do NOTHING to make an extra $6,643.88 except let your money sit there. We could have been doing something else with our money instead of letting it sit in our savings account: invested it elsewhere (in stocks and bonds), spent it on goods (clothes), or put it towards a larger purchase that could also serve as an investment platform (a home).

Economists call the choice among these alternatives *opportunity cost*: the decision to forego certain risk (e.g. in a volatile stock market) or pleasure (the new shoes) in exchange for the security of a secure – if dull – place to park your money. Opportunity cost is as much a psychological measure as it is a quantifiable one: many people tend to like to reward themselves now, rather than defer that pleasure by saving money for what can seem a distant future use (or necessity).

Currently we live in an extremely low rate environment. However, earning .05% on your money is better than earning 0%. Regardless of if you are a Patient Patty or an Anxious Annie, I hope you can see how interest works and how it can make you a decent sum of money. The more money you invest, the more compound interest you will accumulate.

TOPIC #3: SUPPLY & DEMAND

Supply and demand is one of the most important concepts in dealing with the economy. Demand is how much (quantity) of a product or service is desired by buyers. Supply represents how much the market can offer of this product or service. Keep in mind the two laws stated below are theoretical.

Law of Demand. The law of demand basically says that in theory, the higher the price of a good, the less quantity will be demanded.

Law of Supply. This goes backwards from demand. This law states that the higher the price, the higher the quantity supplied. This makes sense because the company making the product will profit more on higher priced goods. On the same hand, the smaller the supply, the higher the price will be.

Here is an example. Think back to college football weekends. At my alma mater, Ole Miss, hotel prices would vary based on the game. For the game against a weak, non-conference opponent, hotels in Oxford might fetch $150/ night. For a game versus a large SEC in-state rival, hotel prices could be double that at $300/ night. The hotels will raise prices because there is an intense demand for these weekends, which increases competition, therefore hotels can create a larger profit.

Examples really help me understand things so here is one more. When Target came out with their Lilly Pulitzer line, it sold out in minutes. Within an hour there were thousands of eBay listings asking $900 for a shirt that sold in stores for $40. That is an unbelievable mark up in price, but the limited supply had been exhausted. Once it sold out, it was gone. Therefore people who REALLY wanted that shirt would have to weigh their option to pay an ungodly markup or simply have to live without the item because the supply had been depleted.

An "opportunity cost" also lies behind the decision not to get up before the sunrise to stand in line at a Target and fight the crowds – still with no promise that the item you wanted would be on the racks by the time you ran through the store; people subconsciously put a value on the time and effort that would have been required to *perhaps* find the Lilly Pulitzer items they wanted, and then decide, effectively, how much extra they are willing to pay someone else to have done the shopping for them (but, again, with no guarantee that what you want will be listed on eBay). Consumers make these kinds of judgments many times every day – sometimes subtly, and sometimes on a grand scale.

Other market forces make the details of supply and demand far more complex than this, but understanding the general idea is the goal!

TOPIC #4: INFLATION

Inflation is a crucial issue to consider because it impacts your purchasing power: how much your money is actually worth. *Inflation* is an increase in the price of goods and services; the dollar you have today will not be worth as much in the future. Historical inflation rates average about 3% per year.

Inflation is measured by the *Consumer Price Index (CPI)*, which is published by the Bureau of Labor Statistics. We need to return to our discussion of supply and demand to explain this. When demand for a product is greater than the supply (more people want something than is currently being produced), this causes prices to rise.

Think about when there is a food shortage. When there is a cold snap in Florida, the prices for oranges sky rocket because they are not as readily available because the supply has been decreased. Therefore your orange that used to cost $1.29, now costs $1.49 because of the lack of supply. When prices rise, this decreases your money's "purchasing power."

The orange situation would not be due to inflation necessarily but more of a supply and demand issue; the point is to grasp the theory of decreasing purchasing power. However, the increase in the price of oranges between 1960 and 2015, would be inflation related.

How does the government control this? In order to ensure inflation does not get out of hand, the Federal Reserve can either print more money, or stop printing as much money if the country is dealing with "deflation." Since your money is inevitably decreasing in value every year, this is why it is important to grow your money through investments.

Inflation is the same thing that your grandparents are talking about when they say, "when I was your age a pack of gum was $.10." Inflation (as well as other factors) has caused this price to rise year after year.

TOPIC #5: LIQUIDITY

You have possibly heard the term "liquidity" before. No, it does not mean how many times your dollar bills have accidently been through the wash in your True Religion jeans.

Liquidity refers to how accessible your money is.

Cash is obviously the most liquid *asset*; as defined by Investopedia: "a resource with economic value that an individual, corporation or country owns or controls with the expectation that it will provide future benefit." Cash is considered the most liquid because you can access it immediately.

Other assets are not so accessible. Retirement accounts such as a 401(k) tie your money up until you reach a certain age (usually retirement age; around 66); early withdrawal comes with penalties and extra taxes (discussed later). Savings accounts are often illiquid as well. Although your savings account may be in the same account as your checking, it is not as accessible. Withdrawals from your savings account can usually only be made a few times (this varies by bank and the settings you have in place).

15

Your home can also be defined as an illiquid asset. It can be a very lucrative asset and is usually your largest, but if all of a sudden you needed money tomorrow, the chances you could sell your home in 24 hours and receive cash for it is very unlikely.

An individual might have very high **net worth**, however they might not be very liquid. This means a person could have a net worth of $25 million but might have many of their assets tied up in investments such as real estate or their companies, therefore the money they actually "have" could be drastically lower as valuations of properties and businesses fluctuate.

Having certain illiquid assets is important to enjoy handsome returns: the *more* illiquid, the *more* return. Cash sitting in your checking account accumulates 0%. But it is crucially important to have an "emergency fund" that is VERY liquid – e.g. cash.

TOPIC #6: BOOMS & RECESSIONS

The word recession is thrown around quite frequently but there are certain events that must occur at the same time in order for the economy truly to fall into a recession. The basics are this:

Recession. A recession is a significant decline in the economy lasting more than a few months.

Consumer Spending:	DECREASE
Unemployment:	INCREASE
Income:	DECREASE
Stocks:	DECREASE
Interest Rates:	DECREASE

Boom. A boom is more difficult to describe because this is simply a period of expansion in the economy when all seems to be going right.

Consumer Spending:	INCREASE
Unemployment:	DECREASE
Income:	INCREASE
Stocks:	INCREASE
Interest Rates:	INCREASE

Interest rates **decrease** during a *recession* in order to incentivize people to borrow money and then spend it in order to revitalize the economy.

Interest rates **increase** during a *boom* because it is now more expensive to borrow money hence making it more profitable to lend money to others.

Booms and recessions both can be predicted fairly well because history has a tendency to repeat itself. Although many events can help to foresee the future of the economy, there are certain events that can happen without notice and put those unprepared in a dangerous financial position.

The main key is to be aware that these events can happen without notice and prepare for the unexpected. Having safe, reliable investments and savings can provide a safety net and lead to less anxiety about the unknown future.

TOPIC #7: CREDIT VS. DEBIT

Most people know credit and debit cards are two different things but don't really know what that difference is. Both have 16-digit numbers, expiration dates, a security code and – most importantly – you can online shop with them. But how does each one function?

Credit card. Credit cards are those things that the clerk at Bloomingdale's offers you in order to save 20% on your purchase today. With a little personal information, social security number, address, etc. you now have a new piece of hard plastic for your wallet and a sweet discount on that DVF wrap dress. But what's the catch? So you just put $260 on this new Bloomingdales credit card. What's interesting is right now you still have that $260 in your bank account...it has not been withdrawn...you have not actually "paid" for your item.

Debit card. A debit card is what you get from your personal bank. It is associated with your checking or savings account into which you deposit money. When you buy that $325 DVF dress (without the 20% store credit card discount), you now have $325 less in your bank account. The money is automatically withdrawn because you are not buying this dress on "credit." A debit card is basically like a checkbook. Debit cards are a direct access to cash that is withdrawn immediately, just like when you write a check and the money is processed from your account. Debit cards are great but will NOT help you establish credit (discussed in a later section).

Credit cards sound fancy and glamorous. How sweet is it that: I get to buy all these amazing new clothes and I don't have to pay for them right now? In theory, yes. The use of a credit card gives individuals a little time to get money for their items. If you don't have a sufficient balance in your debit card at the time of your purchase you either cannot buy it or will suffer an overdraft fee.

The important issue here is you need to be aware of spending money you DON'T have. Many people who have credit cards spend beyond their means because they do not have to pay the charges at the moment. On the other hand, lots of people use credit cards very responsibly.

Many times credit cards are associated with reward or loyalty programs that are an added bonus. For instance, by using the

American Airlines VISA card you earn frequent flyer miles for AA. The more you spend on that card, the more miles you get; (one of the American Airlines credit cards will give you 2 airline miles for every $1 you spend, and that adds up). In order to get one of these cards, you must have established a line of credit – you can't simply apply for one right out of the chute.

Problems with credit cards arise when people spend and spend and spend and then, when their statement arrives at the end of the month, the $940 they have in their bank account can't cover the $1,450 charges they made throughout the month. This affects your credit score.

All credit cards have what is called an ***Annual Percentage Rate (APR).*** This is the percentage charged on the balance if the full amount is not paid before the monthly due date. This sneaky little charge can add up fast if you're unable to pay your bills.

TOPIC #8: CREDIT SCORE

A credit score is probably something you have heard about on commercials, but do you really know how important it is to your financial strength?

First of all remember our discussion about what *credit* is: "the ability of a customer to obtain goods or services before payment, based on the trust that payment will be made in the future." Basically, get your stuff now, pay for it later. But how does the person you are buying from know you will be able to pay them back? By pinky swearing you will?

Unlike promising in middle school that you will pay your friend back for the dollar you borrowed to buy a Coke, in the grown up – or what I like to call "real people" – world, the reliability of your promise to repay comes in the form of a credit score.

A *credit score* is the measure of an individual's creditworthiness. There are numerous factors that go in to determining this number. This number that is calculated is known as your FICO score and is calculated based on these items:

• Payment history;

• Your current level of indebtedness (credit cards outstanding, student loans, car loans);

• Types of credit used and length of that credit.

A credit score falls on a scale between 300 and 850. In general, a FICO score above 650 is good and you will be able to obtain what is known as a *prime* rate. If your score is below 650 then you will have difficulty in securing financing at a favorable rate and will only be able to obtain what is known as a *subprime* rate; these rates will be higher than prevailing rates because you are more of a credit risk.

ESTABLISHING CREDIT

Straight out of college, most of you probably do not have credit. Any credit cards you have probably are not in your name. Also, some student loans may not be in your name either. If they are, then hopefully you have been making your payments on time in order to get your credit score off to a strong start!

If you haven't already done this...the time to start is now!

The key to establishing credit is starting small. Your options can include trading out your debit card for a credit card or borrowing a small amount of money. For instance, my friend got a new car for graduation. Where her parents could have simply paid for her car outright, they decided to finance it in her name, so she has a monthly loan to pay on the car in order to establish her credit.

When establishing this credit it is VITAL to pay off your bills when they are due. By paying on time, you are showing future lenders that you are a viable borrower. If you pay late, this will show up on credit reports. Every missed payment is tracked and can hurt you down the road. Adverse information stays with you for a long time (six years in most cases).

Make sure to keep your charges well within your **credit limit**: the maximum amount the lender (the credit card company) will allow you to borrow at any point in time...they set this for you initially. If you are spending more than your limit it may signal to creditors you have issues controlling your spending that could leave you unable to repay the debt as agreed.

A little nervous you will spend, spend, spend and then be stuck when your payment is due? A secured credit card is for you then. A secured credit card is tied to a separate account you set up. You put a certain sum into this account and then you can charge up to that amount. This will place a bit of a buffer layer in case you overspend.

After you have used a secured card, you can graduate to a regular credit card. After this you can eventually increase your credit card limit. This is not to incentivize you to spend more but instead is to continue and strengthen your credit score. Every time you make a proactive decision to enhance your limit, it is reported and will raise your credit score.

Credit is VITAL for most people to make those big purchases: cars, houses, boats, etc. Some are fortunate enough to be able to pay for things in all cash, but this is rare...especially when you're starting out. Take control and begin responsibly establishing your credit now!

The way a loan contributes to your credit score is slightly different than a credit cards effect. With a credit card you have a "limit" you need to live within; for a loan, you have a large amount your must pay back over time. By paying back your loan on time and staying within your credit limit; your credit score increases.

YOUR FIRST CREDIT CARD

A good card to consider if you are exiting college with little to no credit is the **Capital One Secured MasterCard.** This card is a great way to prove your creditworthiness without lots of hidden fees, and will allow you to establish your credit so you can move up to rewards cards so you can begin earning perks via your spending. Keep in mind that every credit card you APPLY for is documented and will lower your credit score, incrementally.

Apply for one and then work hard to stay on top of it and you'll be earning points with a high-flying card in no time!

TOPIC #9: LEVERAGE & LOANS

Most people know what a loan is, but there are numerous concepts that accompany a loan that some may have trouble processing. A large part of loans are the "interest rates" we discussed above.

A loan is an arrangement when a *lender* gives money to a *borrower*. The lender could be a bank or an individual, and the borrower would be you. Say you needed $50,000 to start up your new business. You may have $50,000 in your bank account but you need that money to pay your bills. You need extra money to invest in your business so you commission a lender. Now in order for the lender to part with his or her money, you must give them something in return: interest payments.

Usually there is a predetermined point in time at which the face value of the loan is due. *Face value* is how much money you borrowed.

There are 3 parts to getting a loan:
1) At the beginning of the loan application process you will need to authorize the release of your credit report to your

potential lender; this includes information such as how many times you have applied for credit, outstanding loans, etc.

2) As emphasized, a high credit score will enable you to get a favorable interest rate on a loan. A low credit score may hinder your ability to finagle a favorable rate – or even to obtain a loan in the first place. You can obtain your credit report at no charge via numerous websites – a popular one is **creditkarma.com**.

3) In order to get a loan you must prove that you have a stable source of income. You will need to bring bank statements or paystubs when applying. The more stable your income (meaning you have a regular job) the more favorable your rate will be.

FINANCING

Taking out a loan is also known as *financing* something; you are buying it on credit. You will be billed periodically along with an interest charge.

I shop quite a bit on a luxury designer consignment website, **TheRealReal.com**. TheRealReal has recently started offering a financing method. Here is how it works. Say I am looking to purchase a Cartier Love ring for $2,500. I have $2,500 in my bank account but this month I also have to pay rent, buy groceries and gas, etc. therefore I would rather not fork out the whole $2,500 right now, so I decide to finance the ring instead.

I have 3 options: 3, 6 or 12 monthly payments with rates from 10-30% APR (APR, or "annual percentage rate," is just like an interest rate but whereas interest rates do NOT include extra fees that may be tacked on...APR is all encompassing and includes all charges).

When you choose this option on TheRealReal, you will have to enter into a contract with the finance company (Affirm) that you agree to their terms and that Affirm has authorization to obtain your credit report. With this information, Affirm will decide if you are creditworthy and will also use it to determine your interest rate. If you pay your bills on time, and have a decent credit score, you may lock in a rate as low as 10%. If you are a higher risk it could be as high as 30%.

TOPIC #10: TAXES

So you got your first job. WAHOO! You just signed a contract that, on the surface, will put $35,000 a year in your pocket. What to buy first?! Let's pump the brakes...that $35k will go faster than you think...oh...and you also don't really get $35k. Enter taxes.

Here is an example of how you may be taxed: Sydney is making $35,000 living in New York City and is paid monthly.

Gross Salary (before taxes)	**$35,000**	
Gross Monthly Pay (before taxes)	$2,916.67	
Federal Withholding		($370.31)
Social Security		($180.83)
Medicare		($42.29)
New York State Income Tax		($120.69)
SDI		($2.60)
Net Monthly Pay	$2,199.95	
Net Salary	**$26,340**	

I believe reality is setting in. From that $35,000 salary you were just promised, almost $9,000 will be seized via taxes, leaving you $2,199 to live on...PER MONTH. Given what your life in college currently costs a week – with many of you still on your parent's dime – it may be time to scale back your lifestyle.

The average college graduate in this day and age can expect their first salary upon graduation to be approximately $45,000 (this varies based on your degree and skill level). Your state of residence will determine the amount withheld from your paycheck each month (some states collect no individual income tax; you always pay federal), so where you choose to live can have a massive impact on how much of your salary you get to keep and the lifestyle you will be able to afford.

FILING TAXES: TAX TERMS

So far we've only seen a general breakout of what turns gross pay into net pay (post tax). There are a lot of things that play a role in determining what taxes you pay, so bear with me...you're going to be a confident tax pro soon! Here are some basics of "tax talk."

Withholding Allowances. Even though you do not actually put all of the money you earned in your pocket – or your bank – you do have some control over the amount that evaporates each pay period. Your employer is the one deducting these taxes from your paycheck in order to pay the *Internal Revenue Service (IRS)* the taxes you owe on your income. How does your employer know how much to deduct? Everyone has a different situation, based on how you fill out your W-4 form. More withholding allowances = LESS income tax your employer withholds (you get to keep more)...and vice versa. These questions include your relationship status, number of dependents, number of jobs you hold etc. If you fill out this form to underwithold (you keep more of your paycheck than you should) then you possibly will be charged a penalty by the government (10-20%).

Err on the side of caution when selecting your withholding allowances as the government would prefer to borrow as much of your money as possible paycheck to paycheck and then inevitably that money will come back to you in the form of a tax return.

Gross Income and Taxable Income. You usually don't pay taxes on all of your income. We will get into the nitty-gritty of retirement plans (401(k), IRA, etc.) later but some of those contributions are made with BEFORE TAX dollars. An example is a *traditional 401(k)* plan. If you contribute to a traditional

401(k) plan you will notice that your taxable income is LOWER because an amount has been taken from your paycheck, prior to the assessment of income taxes, and has been added to your retirement plan. Less income = less taxes. This is a good thing, but it doesn't mean this money you've put away for retirement is insulated from the IRS forever: you will pay taxes when you withdraw it (but in many cases less than you might have paid at the time you earned the money to make the contribution).

There are also ways to contribute AFTER TAX dollars to retirement plans – thus avoiding the payment of taxes when you use that money down the road (we will discuss this later).

Tax Brackets. Here is a chart of the 2014-2015 tax brackets. The U.S. has what is called a ***progressive tax system***. This means the more you make, the more taxes you pay. Remember that "Federal Withholding" deduction line on your paystub? This is how that is calculated with the information you provide on your forms:

Rate	Single	Married/Joint	Head of Household
10%	$0-$9,225	$0-$18,450	$0-$13,150
15%	$9k-$37,450	$18k-$74,900	$13k-$50,200
25%	$37k-$90,750	$74k-$151,200	$50k-$129,600
28%	$90k-$189,300	$151k-$230,450	$129k-$209,850
33%	$189k-$411,500	$230k-$411,500	$209k-$411,500
35%	$411k-$413,200	$411k-$464,850	$411k-$439,000
39.6%	$413,200+	$464,850+	$439,000+

Knowing these specific numbers is not necessarily important, but it is important however to have a general idea of what tax bracket your income will put you in. A lot of my friends are starting off making $35,000...so all you need to do is multiply $35,000 x .15 and then that is your tax amount, right? Nope! There is something called a marginal tax rate which taxes your income at different interest rates.

Marginal Tax Rate. This 15% tax bracket which applies to someone with a $35,000 salary is NOT a fixed percentage you pay on your full $35,000.

If you are single this is how your taxes will work with that income: the first $9,225 will be taxed 10% (see above chart), and the remaining $25,775 will be taxed at 15% (the next step in the progressive tax bracket system).

=$9,225 x .10 = $923
=$25,775 x .15 = $3,867

So the total federal tax withheld on $35,000 salary in 2015 for single person= **$4,790** (NOT $5,250).

Let's look at another example. Now you are married and filing with your spouse. Together you earn $85,000. Here are your taxes:

= $18,450 x .10 = $1,845
= $56,450 x .15 = $8,468 ($74,900-$18,450 = $56,450)
= $10,100 x .25 = $2,525 ($85,000 - $74,900 = $10,100)

Total Taxes on $85,000 combined salaries jointly filed = **$12,838** (NOT $21,250).

As you can see what you are really being taxed on is the difference between the dollar amounts in the tax bracket ranges. If you and your husband were making $85,000 and were not taxed "progressively" then your tax bill would be almost $10,000 more if you simply used 25% across the board! Although this bouncing from tax bracket to tax bracket may seem confusing, it results in lower total taxes!

The taxes will automatically be deducted for you, therefore you don't actually have to go through and divvy out your tax expense this way. However, when planning your yearly or monthly spending, you need to know how much is going to be taken from you via taxes instead of simply guessing. You are now armed and dangerous when you know how to calculate your taxes!

Filing Status. This is fairly self-explanatory but will probably change over the course of your life, so you may need to update your W-4.

1) **Single**. Unmarried and you are the sole person bringing in income this is how you would file. Your imaginary relationship with Channing Tatum does not count. You are still considered single even if you're dating someone. That may seem obvious, but it's good to clarify!

2) **Head of Household**. This filing is for single or unmarried taxpayers who keep up a home for a qualifying person (e.g. a child). This has more breaks than single filing for obvious reasons.

3) **Married**. This is based on your marital status as of December 31st of the tax year. When you are married you have 2 filing options:

  • **Jointly**. This means you and your spouse will file your taxes together. If you make $90,000 and your husband makes $90,000, you would calculate your taxes based on the combined $180,000. This usually saves you money. It all depends on tax brackets (see below).

• **Separately**. This same couple could also file two individual returns based on each $90,000 salary. Here is a layout of how this would work.

If spouses' salaries are similar then filing either way will not make a big difference in the amount of taxes being paid. An example of where this could make a substantial difference would be a couple with vastly different salaries. Let's say the wife is a lawyer making $150,000 and the husband is a professor making $45,000.

Jointly Filing	Separately Filing
Total Salary = ***$195,000***	Total Salary (**Husband**) = ***$45,000***
=$18,450 x .10 = $1,845	=$9,225 x .10 = $923
=$56,450 x .15 = $8,468	=$28,225 x .15= $4,234
=$76,300 x .25 = $19,075	=$7,550 x .25= $1,888
=$98,550 x .28 =$27,594	TOTAL = **$7,045**
=$700 x .33 = $231	Total Salary (**Wife**) = ***$150,000***
TOTAL = **$57,213**	=$9,225 x .10 = $923
	=$28,225 x .15 = $4,234
	=$53,300 x .25 = $13,325
	=$59,250 x .28 = $16,590
	TOTAL = **$35,072** = **$42,117**

In this example this couple could have saved almost $15,000 in taxes by not filing together. Everyone's situation is different and this will be something you and your spouse will need to periodically calculate in order to determine which route will provide you with the best savings.

Now that you understand the basic concepts of your filing status and marginal taxes you can do this on your own when that special person puts a big ole Harry Winston on that ring finger!

Tax Exemptions. (Let me keep my money, Uncle Sam!) Tax exemptions are something everyone likes: these let you REDUCE your taxable income.

> **Personal Exemptions**. If you are single, with no children, and your parents do NOT claim you on their tax forms you can claim this; it will reduce your taxable income by a nice amount.
>
> **Dependent Exemptions**. You can claim a dependent exemption on each person YOU support financially – generally your kids (but other individuals can also count, such as aging parents). Once you start making the BIG bucks though you no longer get this exemption.

Tax Deductions. These are for certain expenses you have paid throughout the year that the government allows you to deduct from you taxable income. **EX**: amount of *interest* paid back on student loans (not principal). You can do this via a Form 1040 Schedule A "Itemized Deductions," on which you list all the expenses you paid during the year that are ELIGIBLE to be deducted from your taxes.

No, the Dior So Real sunglasses from Barneys do NOT count as a tax deduction, sadly. Here is a list of what does:

- State and local income taxes (different states, different rates; discussed later)
- Property tax paid on your home
- Interest paid on mortgage
- Donations to charity (when you take your middle school Hollister polo shirts to Goodwill and they ask you if you want a receipt...the answer is YES!)
- Out-of-pocket medical expenses
- Job search expenses
- Out-of-pocket work related costs (your cell phone, computer)
- Home office costs (Schedule C)

You can either list ALL of these things, or you can simply take a standard deduction if this is too much effort. Just starting off, it is usually simpler to just use the standard deduction.

However, listing all of this stuff out, while tedious, can save you lots of money so you can buy two pairs of those Chanel flats –even though you probably shouldn't. It is also important to note that many of these deductions have complex limitations that you will need to consider.

Tax Refunds. Your regular withholding payments usually result in payment of more than you need to the IRS, so after you file your taxes (by April 15th each year) you will get a pretty little check in the mail from the US Department of Treasury: a "tax refund." If you are getting massive checks you may want to adjust the number of exemptions you claim in your W-4. However, remembering our discussion above, it is better to overstate how much the government should take from your paycheck than to understate to avoid penalty taxes.

TAX PREPARATION

Getting everything together to file your taxes is half the battle; organization is the key to keeping your sanity. Here are the forms you need to fill out and keep in a sacred tax folder:

- W-2 from your employer
- 1099-MISC for self-employment → you'll receive one of these if you do any type of work as an independent contractor; e.g. something you are not formally "employed" by someone to do.
- 1099-INT (interest) and 1099-DIV (dividends) forms. You'll get these if you have taxable investments (stocks and bonds); if you aren't invested in anything or receiving any type of interest you don't have to worry about these.
- 1099-B → these forms will come to your mailbox if you have brokerage trades in stocks and bonds.
- 1098-E → interest paid on student loans.
- 1098 → interest paid on mortgage.
- Documentation showing deductions; receipts from Goodwill donations, medical expenses and contributions to your IRA or 401(k) retirement accounts.

TOPIC #11: SOCIAL SECURITY

Each month that little chunk of change deducted from your paycheck – usually labeled "**FICA,**" which includes your contributions to both the Social Security and the Medicare trust funds – is your unavoidable participation in the retirement plan overseen by the government. Social Security also provides survivor's benefits: if your spouse dies, you can collect their social security when they would have reached retirement age.

Not all people choose to put money away for retirement, but with Social Security you don't have a choice. Social Security helps retirees continue their lifestyle after they stop getting their monthly paycheck, but the amount many people receive from monthly benefits checks is not nearly enough to pay all of their expenses after retirement, so it is vital for you to have other personal savings accounts as well.

You must work a minimum of roughly 10 years (a total of *40* "credits") to be able to draw retirement benefits (see **SSA Publication 05-10072**). There is a simple formula that determines this eligibility. Currently, you receive *1* "credit" for every **$1,220** in gross earnings, but you can accumulate no

42

more than *4* credits per year (in other words, you only need to earn **$4,880**/year to have that count as a full year of employment). This means that most of us who had summer jobs in high school or part-time jobs in college will already have made some headway toward those 40 credits!

The social security tax (12.4% in 2015) is split between you and your employer: you pay half and your employer pays half. If you are *self-employed* then you pay the full 12.4% by yourself. The Medicare tax is an additional 2.9%*. FICA taxes are only collected on the first **$118,500** (in 2015); while the tax rates are slow to change (Social Security and Medicare have stayed the same since 1990), the upper limit of earnings subject to FICA changes almost annually and will surely continue to do so over the course of our working lives.

For comparison's sake, just 20 years ago you stopped making your contribution to the Social Security trust fund once your earnings reached $61,200 (1995); if we look back 10 more years your maximum taxable earnings were only $39,600 (1985); and if we look back a total of 40 years – roughly to the time when people who can begin to retire in 2015 first started their working lives – the maximum earnings subject to FICA were just $14,100 (1975).

One dollar in 1975 has equivalent buying power of $4.42 in 2015, so that $14,100 earnings cap equals roughly $62,333 in 2015 dollars – a far cry from the $118,500 that is subject to Social Security taxes today.

While inflation, life expectancy, and other economic and actuarial factors all play into how the government decides to expand the taxable base for Social Security, it's easy to see how the Treasury Department struggles to take in enough revenue to keep the Social Security system afloat.

We can't get through an election cycle without the future of Social Security coming up for debate. It's impossible to guess how the program will change over the next four decades, but the situation may not be as grim as we hear on the news. In a recent *New York Times* discussion, Josh Barro argues that Social Security "could be made permanently solvent by raising [the 12.4%] tax by two percentage points, or by keeping the tax rate the same and abolishing the cap" ("Living Longer is Great, Except for Social Security," *New York Times*, 11/17/15,

A3). This should give us some hope that we'll see the return of these FICA withdrawals in the future.

The rules governing the distribution of Social Security benefits will also continue to change (perhaps radically) over the next four decades. Today you can begin to receive retirement checks at age 62, but that decision substantially reduces the benefits you'd receive if you continued to work for four more years (the current "full retirement age" is 66). Moreover, your benefits increase at a greater rate if you work past the age of 66, but they max out once you reach the age of 70.

Just as there is a limit to how much of your earnings are subject to Social Security withholding (the first $118,500), there is also a limit to the maximum benefit you can receive each month. Today the maximum benefit payable to someone who retires at age 66 is $31,956 annually, which drops to $24,300 if you retire at 62 and increases to $42,012 if you work to age 70.

What would the difference be for three people with identical job histories who retired in 2015 after turning 62, 66, and 70? Let's say the person at full retirement age will receive

$1,224/month (this is the average size of a Social Security check in 2015); benefits for the person who retires four years younger will be 25% less (only $918/month), while the person who works an extra four years enjoys a 32% boost in benefits (up to $1,617/month).

Despite the fact that working those extra eight years will increase your monthly check by over three-fourths, typically only 1 to 2% percent of retirees work until they turn 70 – and about two-thirds of the population starts to draw benefits before full retirement age (Laurence J. Kotlikoff and Robert C. Pozen, "Let Older Americans Keep Working," *New York Times*, 8/15/15, A19).

So...how long do you have to hope to live to recoup your Social Security contribution? Let's look at someone who took a great job right out of college in 1972, has continued to rise through the ranks of the company, and has decided to retire in 2015 at age 66. Let's also imagine that person always earned at least the maximum salary taxable for FICA purposes (which was only $9,000 in 1972 – the equivalent of roughly $51,200 today – and the rate was then 9.2%). Over the course of those 44 years of employment this person has contributed approximately $242,687 (in inflation-adjusted 2015 dollars) to her Social Security account, and her employer has matched that. So this hard-working retiree and her employer have together put almost *half a million* dollars into the US Treasury for her golden years. Under the rules currently governing the maximum annual withdrawal for someone who retires at age 66, she will receive roughly $32,000/year in Social Security.

At that rate her contributions to Social Security will be repaid in about 7 years, and when we add her employer's matching contribution this means that if she lives past the age of 80 she will start to receive more in Social Security benefits than were ever contributed in her name.

TOPIC #12: RETIREMENT

According to the government's *Retirement Benefits* pamphlet,
"financial experts say you'll need *70-80%* of your
preretirement income" to live comfortably, but "Social
Security replaces only about *40%* of preretirement income for
the ***average*** worker" (**SSA Publication 05-10035**). And
remember, the maximum annual Social Security benefit is
$42,012.

It's fair to ask just what "average" may mean in this context.
In 2012 median personal income was approximately $27,000,
and average personal income was about $41,000. For the
2013 tax year the mid-point Adjusted Gross Income for all
returns was $36,841; an AGI of $127,695 would put you in the
top 10% (see "SOI Tax Stats – Tax Stats at a Glance,"
www.irs.gov).

Let's assume you are very much *above* average, and have just
decided to at the age of 66, and your last year's salary was
$125,000. The guidelines of the Social Security Administration
suggest you can replace 40% of your salary – in this case,
$50,000 – with your Social Security benefits. But remember
that there is a maximum annual benefit if you retire at age 66:

about **$32,000** (and only then if you've been making maximum contributions for four decades*). In this case Social Security will only replace about 25% of your last salary. Operating under these same SSA guidelines, 70%-80% of your pre-retirement salary would be $87,500-$100,000, so you will have to supply an additional $55,500-$68,000 from other sources to maintain your lifestyle.

The higher your salary, the less your Social Security benefits will buoy your retirement years. You will need to plan ahead to make up this difference!

According to Tara Siegel Bernard, "The typical family whose head of household is between the ages of 55 and 64 – and fortunate enough to own a retirement account – has a median balance of just $104,000" ("How to Stretch Savings Without Working Longer," *New York Times*, 8/8/15, B1). Professor Edward Wolff of New York University is blunt is his assessment: "people at nearly all levels of income distribution have undersaved": "Social Security is going to be a major, and maybe primary, source of income for people, even for some of those close to the top" (quoted by Jeff Sommer, "For

Retirees, a Million-Dollar Illusion," *New York Times*, 6/9/13, BU4).

Alicia Munnell, of the Center for Retirement Research at Boston College, agrees: "Most people haven't saved nearly enough, not even the people who have put away $1 million" (quoted by Sommer, *New York Times*, 6/9/13, BU1).

It is never too early to start saving for retirement. It can be a small amount that you don't even notice goes missing each month. You can have an amount ($200) withdrawn from your checking account each month and put in to savings now so it is earning interest. How much would that rack up? Over 43 years that would tally $103,200. If we assume a return of 2% (which is ambitious), your total savings would be $164,406 (with compounding interest). That may not seem too impressive in the grand scheme of things, but it is a miniscule amount to tuck away each month as a little nest egg.

Your salary will fluctuate, as will your expenses, so you will have to be prepared to tailor your approach to savings. Once you start saving, when should you take some of it out and invest it in something that might bring you more than standard interest rates? It depends on your appetite for risk. Let's discuss the different options you have for investing, so you will be better positioned to make an educated decision and get the most bang for your buck!

401(k) PLANS

401(k) plans are the most well-known type of retirement account. Here is how it works. A 401(k) is a way for you (as an employee) to contribute money to an account for your retirement. There are numerous different options to this plan and your employer usually will contribute in some way (sometimes going so far as "matching" your contribution dollar-for-dollar). The numbers of employers that contribute to employee's retirement plans has decreased in recent years and is an important benefit to look into.

When you are considering job offers one of the most important benefits to consider is the 401(k) plan available to you. An employer willing to "match" your contributions is giving you a great head start on your retirement! There are always stipulations involved, though.

Let's say you make $100,000 a year and you contribute 3% ($3,000) a year to your 401(k). If your employer "matches" what you put into this account, at year's end you would have $6,000 in total contributions! Sometimes companies require you to be with them for some time before they are willing to throw money your way: this is called waiting to be "vested." This basically means the employer wants to see that you have a solid interest in staying with the company, so they reward loyalty and avoid giving a transient employee a benefit that is undeserved.

How much can you contribute per year? As of 2015 you can contribute a maximum of $18,000 a year to your 401(k) (this does NOT include the portion your employer matches). It is highly unlikely you will be contributing an amount even close to this as you begin your career because for a lot of us that would be over half of our salary – a girl's gotta eat!

Taxes on your 401(k) – there are two options here.

Traditional 401(k). When you join a company you elect to participate in their 401(k) program or not. Most companies offer this, however not all do. It is important to note some employers REQUIRE their employees participate. If your company does NOT, then you can invest in an individual 401(k).

When you elect to participate you can choose the amount you would like to invest, and you can tweak this amount as you go along. So let's say again you are making $100,000 and decide to contribute $3,000 a year in a traditional 401(k), this $3,000 would be deducted BEFORE taxes are taken out so this LOWERS your taxable income. Basically you are getting to save this money tax-free. However, Uncle Sam always comes to collect. When you hit retirement age and want to withdraw your money, you will then be taxed.

Roth 401(k). This is the type of 401(k) I recommend for ambitious people our age. It is different than a traditional 401(k) in that the $3,000 you are contributing is deducted AFTER you've paid taxes. If you are making $100,000 and choose to invest $3,000, your taxable income will still be $100,000 NOT $97,000. Therefore when you withdraw this money later in life, you can take it out TAX FREE (yay)!

Getting taxed right now doesn't sound super appealing so why would I recommend getting taxed now instead of later? Remember our discussion about tax brackets? It makes sense that as you go through life you will move up in tax bracket status because (hopefully) each year you will be making more and more money. Right now you are in a lower tax bracket than you will be in the future. Therefore, to have taxes taken now instead of later when you will be taxed more is actually a benefit to you. The other side to this is you will be living on less when your income is at its lowest- not always easy. Everyone's situation is different and you must determine which route is the best financial decision for you.

Starting to invest in your 401(k) now is important because of the compound interest we've discussed! The returns on your original investments will add to your nest egg in your account and in turn make you more and more money for retirement!

INDIVIDUAL RETIREMENT ACCOUNTS

Individual retirement accounts are also known as IRAs. An *IRA* is something anyone can invest in regardless of whether or not his or her employer sponsors a retirement program.

If you are working for a company that does not offer a 401(k) program, you can choose to open an IRA and invest either in the traditional or Roth form; exactly the same concept in 401(k) plans (traditional is tax deferred and Roth is taxed now). There are certain stipulations as to who can open a Roth IRA, however.

An IRA is beneficial to many people that are possibly self-employed or simply may work for a small company unable to offer a retirement plan. If you do work for a company in this realm, an IRA can offer you the tax advantages many people receive from contributing to their 401(k) plans.

Annual contribution limits to IRAs tend to be smaller. For 2015 the maximum for people under 50 was $5,500 (if you are over 50 the maximum increases to $6,500).

TOPIC #13: STOCKS

Oh, the glamour of the stock market. Wall Street and handsome men in suits running wild, making millions of dollars, is probably what comes to mind. It is still what comes to mine. *Wolf of Wall Street*, am I right?

The stock market is an excellent way to invest your extra cash and create more wealth for yourself.

Stocks are essentially fractional pieces of ownership in a company. Stocks are issued by corporations (Under Armour, IBM, Hewlett-Packard, etc.) and are traded on exchanges. Companies issue stock to acquire more money for new investments; usually to simply expand the company in some way.

When a company "goes public" for the first time – which means the general public is able to buy shares of the stock – it is called an ***Initial Public Offering (IPO).*** An important note is if you work for a public company, many times your bonuses' and retirement perks will come in the form of stock options. A ***stock option*** is an offer given by a company to an employee to buy company stock at a discounted price.

You make money on a stock if it produces a ***capital gain***. A capital gain would occur if you bought 20 shares of a stock at $10 a pop and then sell at $20. In this instance you have a capital gain of $200 plus the $200 you initially invested. There is a specific capital gains tax you pay on your earnings.

Some stocks also pay ***dividends*** – usually four times a year. Dividends vary from company to company, but they are a fixed amount rather than a fixed percentage of the stock's value. For instance, I just bought shares of the stock ConocoPhillips for $59.53 a share, and this pays quarterly dividends of $.73 a share. It does not seem like a lot in the grand scheme of things, but the more shares you own the more you make.

In addition, the dividend payments come to you whether the stock's price goes up or down (though companies experiencing difficulties may reduce their dividends – or eliminate them altogether), so you are always earning something tangible while you watch the ticker prices over time. You will also have the option to reinvest these dividends – you will automatically "buy" additional shares of the same company with each quarterly payment – or you can take them as a cash deposit to your investment account. *NOTE: not all stocks pay dividends.

Although an investor can receive handsome capital gains from a stock, the stock price also could tank and the investor may decide to sell at a **capital loss**. There are numerous things that can influence the price of a stock besides the strength of the company's earnings statements – or the public's opinion of the company. In a following segment I will recommend my favorite investing platform for venturing in to the stock market as well as discussing the different **indexes** and types of markets. It is important to be familiar with some basics of the stock market.

A **stock exchange** is a market where securities (stocks) are bought and sold. Here are two of the most well known.

New York Stock Exchange (NYSE). This is the place you see on the news and in movies, with people running around frantically and yelling as they places orders over the phone. Although this still happens today, most trading is done electronically. When companies are listed on the NYSE, it means they are very credible. In order for a company to be on this exchange they must be of certain size and pass certain tests.

NASDAQ. The NASDAQ is the second largest exchange, and home to lots of tech firms (though there are also many are on the NYSE). The NASDAQ is different from the NYSE because it is ALL electronic. "Dealers" place stock orders all online; there is no physical location.

Stock indices measure the value of a section of the stock market, and are mainly used to compare how stocks are doing on average.

S&P 500 is the most well-known stock index. It is used as the benchmark for the overall U.S. stock market. The S&P includes 500 companies chosen to reflect the economy as a whole, and offers a broad measure of the health of the stock market.

Dow Jones Industrial Average (DIJA) is better known as the "Dow." This index is made up of the 30 LARGEST publically traded companies listed on stock exchanges (such as Apple and General Electric). When people say the "market" is up today they are generally referring to the Dow. It is important to note not all stocks in the Dow are weighted equally. There are complex formulas that determine this but just know that although the Dow is approximately 17,600...that does NOT mean you divide by 30 and that each stock is worth $600.

The Dow Jones is made up of the 30 largest blue chip companies. *Blue chip* companies have large market capitalizations (lots of money on their balance sheet, based on the value of outstanding shares of stock) and have stable earnings history. Both of these basically mean that these companies have a track record as good investments. This does **NOT** mean you are guaranteed to make money on these stocks, but they certainly are viable companies.

If you have seen Wolf of Wall Street, Leo DiCaprio was trading what are known as *pink sheets.* He was making tons of money (illegally) by telling his clients they were buying *blue chip* stocks and instead being given "pink sheets." He was basically talking up these companies to make them sound viable. This was of course before you could get online and find any amount of information you wanted before making your investment.

If and when you choose to begin investing in the stock market, you can look at this index to see how the market as a whole did for the day instead of needing to look at each stock price to see if it went up. You finally get to use that cool little stock app on your phone...looking smart and sexy!

READY TO INVEST?

The stock market is risky. High risk, high reward is ever prominent here. NONE of your investments made in the stock market are guaranteed. I am going to walk you through the platform I use to invest then give an example of how this works.

When I was 20 I set up my own **Capital One Sharebuilder** account. I highly recommend this. You can download the simple app and have it on your home screen to check how your "portfolio" is looking.

What you need to get going? Proof of who you are (your license and social security card) and seed money (deposited from your bank to your investment account). Once you have done this you will have an account set up.

You will have a dock where you can see how much money is in your account (total of your stocks and cash) as well as how much you have in your account available to be invested. Now you are ready to invest. But what company fits your goals? This is where research comes in.

There are numerous viable companies, but just because a company is big or has performed well in the past doesn't mean it will in the future. Before investing you should Google, Google, Google. Read analyst reports (these people watch stocks and offer their opinions about whether they think the stock is going to go up in price or down), pay attention to current events and most importantly only invest within your means.

Let's say you have some spare cash and you want to try to make a little money off of it. You have $1,000 to invest so you decide to buy shares of Intel. If its price is at $21.03, you can then purchase 47 shares (you can only buy whole shares of stocks, while you can buy fractional shares of mutual funds). This will cost you $988.41. In the "action" section you would click "buy" to purchase your stocks. You will then enter the *ticker symbol*; this is the way stocks are known on the exchanges (basically one-, two-, three-, or four-letter abbreviations). For example, Apple is AAPL and Starbucks is SBUX. You will then enter the number of shares you desire to purchase.

After you complete this, the system will ask you to confirm the transaction and then, once you execute the trade, it will give you a receipt. You will be charged a fee in order to complete the transaction. I prefer Sharebuilder because they only charge you $6.95 for each transaction (whether you are buying or selling).

You now own 47 shares of Intel. You can hold on to these stocks as long as you would like. I keep each of the companies I am invested in on my stock app just so I can check on them each day and track if I am up or down.

DAL	43.85	− 0.25
UA	96.14	+ 0.09
COP	50.73	− 1.36
SBUX	56.99	− 0.30
AAPL	122.70	− 1.80
SPY	206.47	− 1.53
BP	35.90	− 0.67

Smart players will be taking small bites of Big Oil Forget about picking a bottom in oil or it...
at MarketWatch - 8:01 AM

China Court Allows NGO's Oil-Spill Lawsuit Amid Pollution Fight A Chinese court allowe...
at Bloomberg - 6:07 AM

What Is The E&P Industry Outlook, Coming Out Of 2QFY15? Bidness Etc takes a look a...

YAHOO!   Real Time Price

When you click on the stocks, this app also pulls up articles related to the company, which can provide forecasts of how analysts think the stock is going to perform. It is a good mechanism to know when to keep your stock or when to sell it!

As you can see above, these are the stocks I am invested in. I keep a mental note of how much I paid for these stocks and then can track their progress throughout the day. Delta Airlines (DAL) has a red box next to it with -.25, which means the stock price is down $.25 for the day. Under Armour (UA) is green with a +.09, meaning the stock is up $.09 for the day.

Under Armour just released a positive quarterly earnings report, and this often leads to a nice bounce in the stock's price. Though sometimes companies make substantial profits, they may fall short of estimates (what their profits etc. had been predicted to be by analysts), so their stocks' prices actually fall even though they are not losing money.

Sometimes there is no rhyme or reason for the way stocks react to outside factors. A large factor that influences stocks is what other investors are doing. If there is a large market selloff (lots of people getting rid of/selling their interest (stock) in a company) because of *investor fears;* recently it was the Chinese stock market tanking; then this massive selloff by people that own shares of your same stock can cause the stock price to fall rapidly.

Clearly, we cannot control or predict global events such as this and of course have ZERO control over what other investors choose to do with their investments. The unknowns simply reemphasize the risk that comes with investing in the stock market.

Investing is invigorating and being able to make money off your money is a GREAT feeling. If you desire to learn more about it I encourage you to read the finance section of the *Wall Street Journal*, online blogs, Barron's financial journal as well as market experts such as Jim Cramer to become better informed. But you should approach investing with caution.

Many people have lost LOTS of money trying to bet big in the stock market. This should be used to help grow your nest egg, not risk it. The stock market is essentially like Vegas...throw your money down on the table, you may walk away with more or you may walk away with less. My dad has always referred to it as "legalized gambling," which essentially is the big picture.

Warren Buffet is one of the most famous investors in the world and his philosophy is one many people follow. He advises investors to "invest in what you know/use." For example, if you drive a Ford, buy Ford stock; if you wear Under Armour athletic apparel, buy Under Armour stock.

TOPIC #14: BONDS

A **bond** is a fixed income debt security. A **fixed income security** is an investment vehicle that pays a regular (non-fluctuating) interest or coupon payment (can also be in the form of a dividend).

Bonds generally are safer than stocks because they make guaranteed interest payments (as discussed above). An interest payment is the bond issuer's compensation to you, the lender, for parting with your money for a fixed period of time.

To whom are you "lending" this money?

>   **Governments:** U.S. government/treasury, federal agencies, other countries (Greece), states.
>   **Municipalities:** cities (used to improve roads, infrastructure, schools).
>   **Corporations:** these function much like stocks; this is essentially a company borrowing money.

In return for your loan, the issuer provides you with a bond, which is a promise to pay a specified rate of interest during the life of a bond when it comes due. As stated above, right now interest rates are VERY low, so your return on a bond generally will not be too impressive – but the risk is much less than in the stock market (for the most part.) There are things known as **junk bonds**, which are very risky bonds, but these usually pay a higher interest rate.

The safest bond is issued by the U.S. Treasury and is backed by the federal government; this bond has very little **default risk**: the possibility that you will not receive your money back when the bond has matured. This can happen from things such as municipal or corporate bankruptcy. Treasuries (T-bonds), however are considered safe because they are essentially insured by the U.S. government.

BONDS & INTEREST RATES

Rising interest rates are BAD for bonds. That seems counterintuitive, right? So why would that be? Say you buy a bond for $1,000 and it pays 2.5% (whenever we give a percentage it means that is what the bond pays *ANNUALY*) and matures in 10 years (the maturity date is when you get the **face value** of your bond back...the $1,000.) You will make $25 each year for a decade, so your total return will be $1,250. Your $1,000 bond at 2.5% is its **par value**.

This 2.5% interest rate here is known as a coupon rate. A *coupon rate* is simply the yield paid by a fixed income vehicle (e.g. a bond). The interest payments made are known as *coupon payments*.

Now assume you decide you need money now. You can't wait 10 years to get your $1,000 back, so you decide to sell your bond and forfeit the future interest payments you would have received. But if the prevailing interest rate at that time has gone up – let's say to 3.5% – and your bond is stuck at 2.5%, you will have to sell your bond for less than face value in order to attract someone who could buy a new bond with the higher interest rate. This means your bond would be selling for "below par."

Happily, the opposite is also true: if interest rates drop during the period you own the bond you can sell it before it matures for more than face value. Your bond would sell for "above par." With this, the bonds new owner then gets to enjoy earning this higher interest – but you have your initial investment back and *then* some.

Although it seems like falling interest rates would be bad for bonds, it is quite the opposite. Although many investors choose to hold on to their bonds until maturity, to receive full face value as well as all interest payments, those who need to get out early may base this decision on current market environment.

RISK & RETURN

You have an option to invest in Treasury bonds for 1-6 months, 1, 3, 5, 7, 10, 20 or 30 years. The interest rate for a 1-year bond is currently 0.34%, which is very low. The interest rate on a 30-year T-bond is 3.08%.

To me, this has always seemed backwards. It may seem that if you were lending your money for longer then the government should pay you a lower percentage because you will be receiving this interest rate payment for longer, but that is not the case.

The longer you part with your money, the longer you have a "locked" in interest rate. Because interest rates fluctuate, your bond having this fixed rate for a longer period of time means more risk to you, hence why longer-term bonds generally have higher interest rates. This is known as *interest rate risk.*

This may not be relevant to you or looking to invest in vehicles such as this but the concept is important to understand.

Fixed income securities can be an excellent source of investment money. Most investors are immediately drawn to the stock market and although the bond market can be difficult to understand, it can also be quite lucrative.

CERTIFICATES OF DEPOSIT

An investment platform VERY similar to a bond is called a certificate of deposit (CD). A *certificate of deposit* is, just like a bond, a *fixed-income security*.

Following the same principle of a bond, when an investor chooses to put their money in a CD they do so for a fixed period of time with the knowledge of how long their money will be tucked away in this investment as well as the return they can expect (the interest/coupon rate). The creditor (you) who is lending money to someone else is given this interest rate in order to compensate for delaying the ability to spend your money.

As seen above in our discussion of bonds, we saw the issuers (the people asking for money) were generally companies, governments and other entities. In the case of CDs, the issuers are **banks**. CDs are considered more of a savings account than anything else. While stocks and bonds are looked at as investment vehicles that can have high returns, CDs are essentially a place to "park" your money for a period of time which can be as little as one month.

Think back to our discussion of checking vs. savings accounts. With a savings account, this money is sitting in your bank earning a low percentage rate but is accumulating risk-free. There is no chance you will lose money from your savings account, you could lose money on a bond.

A CD is the same principle as it is basically a place to store your money until you need to use it for a purchase or find another, more profitable investment.

TOPIC #15: DIVERSIFICATION

A commitment to *diversification* is crucial to successful investing. To have a diverse "portfolio" means you have a wide variety of investments with varying degrees of risk attached to them. Your *portfolio* can be made up of many different things although we will stick to stocks and bonds. Choosing the percentages of vehicles to have in your portfolio is called *asset allocation*.

It is of vast importance to have a well-diversified portfolio between equities and fixed income investments. The stock market is quite risky, therefore if a downturn were to occur, hopefully you would have investments in fixed income assets as well that could potentially offset your loses.

The allocation percentages in your portfolio changes as you get older, but these are the general recommendations:

Age	% Stocks	% Bonds
21-30	70%	30%
40-65	30%	70%

Why should your percentage of stock ownership decrease as you age? When you are young you have more time to make your money, take greater risks, and recover from mistakes and downturns in the market. As you get closer to retirement you want to diminish risk and try to establish predictable returns on your investments with bonds and other safer investments.

Some risk is still fine, but you wouldn't want to find yourself only a few years from retirement and have your savings reduced by half (or worse) if the stock market drops as it did in 2009, leaving many people in that very situation.

TOPIC #16: MUTUAL FUNDS

Think of a *mutual fund* as a "basket" – or mixture – of stocks that are typically keyed to a certain industry (energy, utilities, healthcare) or investment strategy. A mutual fund can contain stocks from any number of companies and are overseen by money managers, which are essentially stock pickers who choose stocks for their funds based on their expertise.

Mutual funds may be a little out of your price range currently, but the main reason to bring the topic up is a question that only 30% of the American population know the answer to...let's see if you get the right answer:

True or False: investing in a single stock is safer than investing in a mutual fund?

This of course is FALSE. Investing $1,000 in a single stock is far more risky than investing in a mutual. If that one company's stock begins having issues with corporate governance, poor earnings reports, etc.; the stock could tank and you would not be very well diversified.

However, if you were to be invested in a mutual (say with 20 different company stocks), if 1 of those was performing badly, you have the cushion of 19 others.

This is essentially the same principle of diversification as discussed in the previous section. The more diverse your stocks are, from varying industries etc., the better positioned you will be if one industry begins having difficulties.

TOPIC #17: MARKET INFLUENCERS

Many people would assume that a stock's price is based on that company's performance. Although this does play a key role, many other things can determine that price.

Things that have a large effect on the stock market have an equal but *opposite* effect on the bond market. When interest rates are LOW, the stock market looks more appealing because there will be a higher return (though there is greater risk). When interest rates are HIGH, the bond market is more appealing because the investor can make more money and risk is diminished.

These factors are complex, but it is important to keep an eye on those issues that affect the entire economy and, in turn, have an impact on your investments and their volatility.

Oil. Oil prices have a HUGE affect on the stock market. Which stocks suffer when oil prices fall? You guessed it, energy stocks. What stocks *SHOULD* benefit from a drop in oil prices? Airlines, trucking; any company that uses oil to conduct business. In theory, lower oil, means lower overall stock prices. However, this is not always the case as seen in current

2015 conditions where oil is at record lows and the market is setting record highs. Just for reference the price of oil in January of 2016 is $29/barrel down from $51 in July.

Unemployment Rate. It would make sense that when the unemployment rate is high; generally speaking stocks are low. Unemployment is a very large indicator of how the economy is doing overall. People have less money to invest and will lean towards safer assets. The AVG unemployment rate between 1948 and 2004 was 5.6%. Unemployment has ranged over the past 60 years from 2.5% to 10.8%. (The formula to calculate the unemployment rate is as follows: Unemployed & Searching for Work / All Individuals in Labor Force.)

Gross Domestic Product (GDP). GDP is the main way to gauge how well the country is doing financially. The rate of GDP in the U.S. has averaged 3.26% from 1947 until 2015. GDP fluctuates each year as different events in the world take place and shape this number. The formula for GDP is made up of the following components: Consumer Spending + Investments + Government Spending + (Exports – Imports).

TOPIC #18: CAR INSURANCE

Wahooooo! Insurance! Everyone's favorite topic.

Insurance is not something we put high on our priority list, but let's face it – it ought to be.

Car insurance is NOT typically covered by your employer. There may be exceptions if, for instance, you have a job that requires you to drive to make deliveries etc.

So what does that little sheet of paper in your glove compartment say? It gives your name (or your parents' names), a description of your car, and your vehicle ID number (VIN), and is called your *Proof of Insurance*. This is what you give the police officer when he pulls you for speeding. All states require drivers to have insurance.

How does this all work? Every policy has something called a *deductible*; this is the amount of money **YOU** will be on the hook for if you are in an accident. There are six components to a car insurance policy:

Comprehensive. This provides coverage for damage done to YOUR vehicle. This includes flood, theft, damage to vehicle by an animal etc. This will be the coverage that will pay for these damages. This is NOT accident coverage.

Crash/Collision. This is for the harm done to YOUR vehicle when you get in an accident.

Physical Injury. This is the coverage that will pay for the injuries you may have caused to the *other party* in the event the car accident was YOUR fault.

Personal Injury. This is known as "no fault" insurance. This is to provide a percentage of YOUR medical, funeral, rehabilitation and lost wages if you are in a car accident regardless of whose fault it was.

Underinsured Motorist. This will help in the event you are in an accident and the other party does not have adequate limits of insurance. For instance, the other party has limits (how much a policy will pay) on their insurance of $1,000 and they caused $1,500 of liability damage to you (not property). This coverage would pay the $500 above their limit.

Uninsured Motorist. This protects you from drivers who do not have any liability insurance. Every driver is required to have insurance although not all do. This protects you because most likely you will never be able to collect any type of reimbursement from these individuals.

Here is an example of how car insurance deductibles work:

> Sydney Hedberg's Car Insurance Policy
> **Deductible**: $1,000
> Damage to car from accident I caused: $2,500
> How much **I PAY**: $1,000
> How much my **insurance company** pays: $1,500

Step 1: When you get in an accident the first thing the parties' involved need to do is exchange insurance information. No matter whose fault it is, both individuals need to do this because your insurance agency is going to take care of settling the payments.

Step 2: File a *claim* with your insurance agency. This means calling the 1-800 number on the back of your card to report an incident. Once the police arrive they will survey the accident and will report their findings to your insurance company.

Step 3: Go to a body shop to determine the total cost of the damage. Many carriers will have certain appraisers they require you to use for an estimate. This is only for your car; you may be responsible for the other driver later but right now this is all about you.

Step 4: Get a quote (how much it will cost) and report this to your carrier (insurance company). You may choose to report this to the insurance company only if it is *over* your deductible. If the quote you receive is $900 and your deductible is $1,000, reporting this to your insurance agency will do nothing except raise your rates! The insurance company will not pay anything for these repairs anyway so you'll be paying out of your own pocket.

Keep in mind if you don't report this to your insurance carrier because the quote was within your deductible, this can also backfire on you. Say the body shop quoted your repair estimate at $900 but when they begin working it actually costs $1,300. Usually you can still report this after but it is important to keep in mind some carriers require you to report at the time of the incident or you will not receive compensation.

Step 5: You will pay nothing as your insurance company will pay for the entire thing right now. At the end of the month, your insurance company will send you a bill for the $1,000 you OWE them (your *deductible,* also known as *retention*). The other $1,500 is ABOVE your *retention.* You pay the $1,000 and your insurance company covers $1,500 to cover the total $2,500 repair. Your insurance will also have a *limit* which is the maximum amount your insurance company will pay for a claim.

If you were not at fault in an accident, through a long process known as *subrogation* your deductible will be refunded to you after the insured at fault's carrier sends payment to your insurance provider.

So what's the catch? Each month in order to get this coverage you pay what is called a *premium;* this is the cost of your insurance, and is TOTALLY different from your deductible. A premium can be thought of as the opportunity cost of insurance (however, you MUST have car insurance). You may go a whole year with no accidents but you still have to pay those $230 insurance premiums every month. The sole reason? It is the law and there are many unknowns – you can't predict when you may need to invoke your coverage. If you chose to not have insurance, you could be sued.

When you are setting up your own insurance policy here are some things to remember:

1) Your insurance premium will be based on your driving record. The insurance company will run a check on your driving history; the more accidents or moving violations you've had, the more that will INCREASE your premium because you are a larger "liability" (more of a risk to the company).

2) The higher your deductible, the LOWER your premium. Think about it. If you are taking on the responsibility of paying for $1,000 of your wreck, this has less impact on an insurance company's bottom line than if you choose to only pay for the first $250.

3) Your *deductible* is on a *per occurrence* basis – EACH time you get in a wreck you are responsible for paying it, so use great caution when evaluating your options. If you have a history of being a bad driver, then these dollar amounts could

add up quickly and severely hurt your budget. Your deductible/retention needs to be well within your budget because you never know when you will get in an accident. If you choose too high of a deductible in order to obtain a lower premium, you may be in financial trouble if you are unable to pay that large deductible.

TOPIC #19: HEALTH INSURANCE

In particular, health insurance can be SUPER expensive – even when you're young – so when considering a job offer it is an important factor to see if the company includes health care coverage as part of your benefits package. If not, you need to ensure you are accepting a salary that is high enough to be able to cover this on your own.

There are a few choices when it comes to ensuring you have health insurance after college. If you have any idea of how much doctors' visits cost, health insurance is DEFINITELY one thing you do not want to be without.

PLAN OPTIONS

Employer-Based Health Insurance. Most Americans obtain their health insurance as a benefit offered by their employers. You should keep this in mind when considering a job offer because health insurance is NOT cheap.

Individually Purchased Health Insurance. The younger and healthier you are, the more affordable health insurance will be. Make sure to shop around before choosing a carrier.

Your Parents' Health Insurance Plan. This is most likely how you've been covered while in college. You are now able to stay on your parents' health insurance plan until age 26. After this you have to fend for yourself.

Short-Term Health Insurance. Let's say you have just turned 26 and are being kicked off your parents' health plan. You are beginning a job in 3 months that offers you health benefits, but going 3 months without insurance is NOT a wise decision. A short-term plan would be your solution. This provides you with temporary insurance if you expect to gain coverage elsewhere (from a job) within the next 6 months.

Government High-Risk Pools. This is where you would go if you have been declined health insurance because of a pre-existing condition (The Affordable Care Act eliminates the pre-existing condition exclusion).

Being Uninsured. TERRIBLE idea. This really is not an option. Health costs are incredibly expensive and generally there would be no way to pay for this all on your own.

As seen in our discussion of auto insurance, health insurance also involves deductibles. A deductible once again is the amount YOU as the patient (the insured) pay before your health insurance will begin to pay. An example would be if you chose a plan with a $1,500 deductible...you will pay the entirety medical service bills until you reach $1,500 for **the year**. Keep in mind this $1,500 is only for **medical service bills**; this does not include pharmacy and prescription drug costs usually. As you will see later, there is a separate deductible on your insurance card that is dedicated to these costs. This is different from a car insurance deductible because this is cumulative not per use.

Once you have paid your deductible for the year, something called **coinsurance** will likely come into play. This means you are still partially responsible for a portion of your medical payments throughout the balance of the year until you reach your plan's out-of-pocket limit. For example, if you elected the $1,500 deductible and by mid-June you have already paid that amount for healthcare, any medical expenses after this will fall into a quota share. When choosing your insurance plans you can also elect what percentage you would like to be responsible for after your deductible.

Let's say you choose a 30/70 quota share. This means you will pay 30% of medical bills and your insurer will pay the other 70%. Once you have paid your $1,500 deductible for the year, let's say you break your leg and it costs $1,000 for x-rays, a cast, and follow-up office visits. According to your chosen plan you will pay $300 and your insurer will pay the remaining $700. What the heck?! I thought I already paid my fair share?! You did – you paid your deductible. One reason coinsurance exists is to keep people from taking advantage of the system. If an individual knows all of their injuries will be covered 100% by insurance, they may choose to be more reckless knowing they will face no financial repercussions.

Co-pays can also be charged when you walk into your doctor's office. Your insurance card will list what your co-pay is for different types of visits. With certain types of insurance the co-pay will be a split percentage between you and your insurance carrier (e.g. 20/80). Here is a typical co-pay breakdown with Blue Cross Blue Shield:

Primary	$25
Specialist	$50
Urgent Care	$50
ER	$150/$200
Rx (Prescription) Deductible	$200

For a *primary care* visit (a simple office visit at your clinic for a standard cold) you will pay $25 (for follow-ups you do not pay, generally). A *specialist* is someone like an OB/GYN or an Ear, Nose & Throat doctor. These doctors are specialists and you are going for a specific reason, so the co-pay is higher. *Urgent care* is that place you have to go after normal clinic hours when you fear you are dying but it's actually just a really bad hangover. This co-pay is more expensive as well because of the convenience. You go to the *emergency room* when something serious happens and is more expensive because such visits typically require much greater deployment of professional resources. If you've ever been to the ER you know how many people are involved in your care, and how many tests you undergo in a very short period of time.

A co-pay is generally required each time, and has nothing to do with your deductible. You always pay the co-pay even if you have reached your deductible limit. Co-pays may also be seen as a kind of mechanism to keep people from taking advantage of the system.

The *Rx* (prescription) deductible is what we discussed above; this is simply how it is listed on your card. In this case, the individual has a $200 deductible meaning the insured is on the hook for $200 worth of prescriptions before insurance will begin paying.

CHOOSING YOUR PLAN

So how are health insurance plans priced? A plan with a HIGH deductible will have lower monthly payments. You are willing to absorb more of the costs, so your insurer takes on less risk.

Remember, choosing a high deductible means you are responsible for all costs up to your chosen dollar amount. If you are relatively healthy and don't have a lot of recurring prescriptions or chronic conditions that need management, you may be better off choosing a plan with a higher deductible.

However, if you have health problems that make you a regular visitor at your clinic, it may be time to change your plan to a lower deductible. The lower a plan's monthly payments, generally the more you will also pay in coinsurance. If you are a slight hypochondriac, then choosing a plan with a low co-pay may be wise so you are not forking out $50 each time you go to see your specialist.

TOPIC #20: LIFE INSURANCE

Life insurance is exactly what it sounds like: it is insuring your life. Right now if you are either in college or a recent graduate, you most likely do not have any dependents so the need for this insurance is not necessary. So when should you think about buying life insurance?

Straight out of college you get a good paying job. Your net worth is steadily increasing and 10 years down the road you get married. As spouses you are now able to take out life insurance on one another because if something were to happen to one of you, your lifestyle would be affected. You may have taken on responsibilities, like a mortgage (there is also mortgage insurance), that requires both of your incomes to support. In order to take out a life insurance policy on someone you must prove dependence; show they provide financial support to you.

If your husband is making $150,000 and you are a stay-at-home mom then the sole lifeline to your family's lifestyle is supported via your husband. If something were to happen to your husband where he could not perform his job anymore, then you all would be able to collect disability. However, God

92

forbid this happens but, lets assume your husband passes away...where will your income come from now? You as the sole adult will now most likely have to find a job in order to provide for your family. Having a life insurance policy in place on your husband will cushion this blow.

A life insurance policy can only be taken out on someone that you rely on financially, your husband for instance. Your husband would name you, his wife, as his **beneficiary**: the person who will receive the benefits in the event of his untimely passing.

The amount of life insurance one is allowed to take out is based on age and on their income. The older one gets, the more life insurance begins to cost because the chance of death increases.

Benefits paid from life insurance are generally used to pay for funeral expenses, medical costs and to help provide a financial pipeline until the family can figure out another source of income.

TOPIC #21: DISABILITY INSURANCE

If you are single and are solely responsible for supporting yourself, it's important to have disability insurance in case you are injured and are not able to perform the duties of your job. Along with Social Security disability benefits, there is the option to purchase disability insurance.

There are two types of disability insurance:

Partial Disability. You are still able to perform your work, but with limitations.

Total Disability. You are not able to perform your work at all.

In addition, disability insurance can run for different durations.

Temporary Disability. You can either be partially disabled or fully disabled for a temporary time period – say for 6 months.

Permanent Disability. You can no longer work at all. For instance, if you are a surgeon and develop Parkinson's you can never operate again.

Hopefully you will never have to use disability insurance. Disability claims are rare for most people performing clerical tasks (working at a desk), but there are instances where your health prevents you from doing even the simplest tasks.

The most important thing to keep in mind is that, when choosing an employer, you should evaluate not only how big your paycheck will be, but also the value of the benefits they offer: both retirement and insurance plans.

TOPIC #22: 50, 20, 30 RULE

In her book, *All Your Worth,* Senator Elizabeth Warren discusses how you should be divvying up your monthly paycheck in order to ensure you are covered for the future.

• **50%** or less should go to your essentials (your recurring expenses: rent, utility, grocery, and transportation to and from work.

• **20%** to the future: emergency fund, retirement, paying down debt (credit cards, loans).

• **30%** to your wants: your leisure activities (going out to dinner, shopping, travel).

For example, if you are making $35,000 a year ($26,340 after taxes) you net $2,195 a month (under the assumption you are single living in NYC). So under our 50/30/20 rule here is the breakdown.

1) **50%** for your essentials equals **$1,096** for groceries, rent, utilities, transportation, etc. WOW! That isn't very much. This shows that when you're starting off you may need to tweak your spending percentages a little if this does not seem realistic – or think about a roommate.

2) **20%** for future savings equals **$439** and also must be allocated for any payments on credit cards you owe or

balances on your student loans. You need to set the amount you will be paying per month based on a percentage such as this one; if you have a large student loan, you may need to increase this percentage.

3) **30%** for wants equals **$659**. This is a fairly large number and can be scaled back until you establish yourself a little more or once you have saved a little nest egg.

It's important to note that these percentages are listed in order of importance. Your essentials are what need to be covered first; if these are not a priority then you will have no place to live, no food and no running water. These expenses come before anything else.

Second when looking toward funding your future you may have to funnel a large part of that percentage toward paying yours debts. It makes sense that the longer you take to pay off your debts, the more it will cost in interest. The most important thing about loans is to pay them off ASAP – you don't want that debt burden hanging over your head for too long.

If you are fortunate enough to have no debt when you graduate, you can think about putting the full 20% of your monthly earnings in your 401(k) or other investments. If you graduate with lots of student debt, your goal should be to live modestly, but this should be true anyway. You may need to sacrifice some of your "wants" in order to retire these loans and escape the burden of living in debt.

Third in your list of priorities are wants. Remember, we work to live, we shouldn't live to work! The trip to Miami for the weekend, the drinks with your girlfriends after work and the bottomless mimosa brunches on Sundays are all "wants" even though we may sometimes argue a weekend of R&R is a need.

Tailoring this spending during times when you do not have as much disposable income is very important. Fresh out of college you most likely will not be living like you were.

Expenses pile up each month, and part of being an adult means you learn to budget and accept that maybe you can't go out and get drinks EVERY night (unless you make friends with a bartender).

Learning to budget in this way will make you savvy and much more cognizant of how much you are actually spending. Devoting $659 each month for whatever you want may seem like a lot, but when you actually break down how much you are currently spending – as we will do in our next section – it will shock you how fast it goes.

Another thing that will surprise you is how much your "essential" life costs. In the following section, we will break down your recurring fixed expenses and your weekly incidental purchases such as visits to the grocery store. Then you will have a better idea of how much you will need to budget. Some people eat less than others therefore your grocery bill is less, however, you may have expensive monthly prescriptions you have to fill.

Another allocation you may like to make would be that for charity. If you have leftover "want" money and have already invested some in retirement etc. a nice place for the excess could be charities.

The worst thing you can do is NOT be prepared. NOT know how much you're spending because it either scares or overwhelms you to think about it and you would rather be naïve. This is a painless way to become more aware. You are not the only one going through this transition period and that's what it is: a transition. This is not permanent.

Through your life you will get higher paying jobs as you become more experienced and become more of an asset to your employer, and with that you can amp up your lifestyle. For now, be smart and learn to be SAVVY.

TOPIC #23: BREAK IT OUT

Knowing how much is in your bank account and what your monthly withdrawals look like is VITAL. Most of you probably have a debit card. When I opened my debit card in high school my dad used it as a training tool. He made us balance every purchase we made and every deposit to ensure we understood the concept of balancing your budget because this is essentially like a checkbook. If you are a rookie at budgeting this would be a good training tool. By jotting down a little note every time you spend, it makes you more aware of what you are spending your money on.

In this section you will need your bank statement from this past month (if this month was a light or heavy month try and choose one that is closer to average for you). It is still important, however, to note occasional big purchases to realize how much you are spending.

Log this information in a chart. At the end put your account total so you know how much money you are currently working with. Hopefully it is a decent amount and not the $25 my sister recently discovered was her balance!

TOPIC #24: MONTHLY RECURRING EXPENSES

As discussed above, these expenses will (for the most part) take up half of what you can spend each month; most of these are NOT wants, but are necessities you need to pay for each month (groceries are not yet included). I'll show you some of my expenses as an example; go through your financial statements (or make estimates if you will start having these expenses soon – there are numerous websites where you can get an idea of these costs).

Monthly Recurring Expense	Amount
Rent	$500
Cable & Internet	$109
Cell Phone	$110
Car Insurance	$302
Gym Membership	$99
Wall Street Journal	$12
Eye Contacts	$30
TOTAL	*$1,161*

TOPIC #25: SEVEN-DAY BREAKDOWN

This is where things are going to become very real for most of us...it definitely did for me. You will need to track your purchases diligently for a whole week. Everything from your cup of Starbucks, to the Wal-Mart run to your grocery purchases...log EVERYTHING.

Within this I would like all of you to do your "big" grocery shopping excursion as well as what I call my "Annoying Wal-Mart Run." This is the trip I absolutely have to make when I am squeezing the top of my toothpaste tube or banging my shampoo bottle against my shower wall to get the last drop. I try to do all of that kind of shopping only once a month; the amount will vary month to month, but it is essential to have a general idea of how much you are spending.

NECESSITY BREAKDOWN

Wal-Mart	Longevity	Groceries	Longevity
Shampoo $6.54	1 month	Chicken $14.56	1 week
Conditioner $6.54	1 month	Lettuce $5.69	1 ½ weeks
Soap $4.26	1 ½ months	Yogurt $9.89	1 ½ weeks
Razor $8.65	1 month	Eggs $3.29	1 week
Toothpaste $4.56	1 month	Cheese $6.78	2 weeks
Toothbrush $3.32	1 month	Bread $4.26	2 weeks
Tampons $12.11	1 month	Peanut Butter $4.65	1 month
Advil $11.60	3 months	Butter $3.89	1 month
Contacts $9.89	3 months	Chips $3.98	2 weeks
		Berries $9.41	1 ½ weeks
		Granola $5.36	1 ½ weeks
		Crackers $3.46	2 weeks
		Soup $9.36	2 weeks
TOTALS	**$67.47**	TOTALS	**$84.58**

Obviously some items last longer than others, but getting all of this in one fell swoop can help you budget. When it comes to groceries, think in a macro view: buy things that you can stretch into several meals.

For instance, I try to bring my lunch to my internship. I cook chicken at the beginning of the week along with veggies. I freeze some of the chicken and then refrigerate the others in separate bowls for the week. This is also a great way to lose weight because it teaches you portion control if you're trying to divvy it up to last you all week! Have a plan when you shop.

7-DAY EXPERIMENT

Mon	Tues	Wed	Thurs	Fri	Sat	Sun
Starbucks $3.43	Starbucks $4.27	Office Depot $15.49	Wal Mart $67.47	Starbucks $3.43	iHop $12.67	Starbucks $3.43
Car Wash $6.00	Groceries $84.58	Dessert $3.97	Liquor $12.45	Bar $16.79	Bar $14.12	
Manicure $15.00				Pizza $4.59	Taxi $10.00	
Panera $13.46						
$37.89	$88.85	$19.46	$79.92	$24.81	$36.79	$3.43
						$291.15

After looking at your necessity purchases as well as how much you typically spend in a week, we now will see how much you have left over within your monthly budget.

As seen below we have the inevitable purchases. Total this to see your remaining funds for the month. Here comes the time when you need to decide which purchases during your week you can eliminate, or at least cut down on (remember those monthly recurring!) Everyone puts a different value of things so this is your time to determine where to trim your spending.

MONTHLY BUDGET

Purchases	Amounts	# of trips/month	TOTAL
Groceries	$84.58	2	$169.16
Wal-Mart	$67.47	1	$67.47
Rent (a portion)	$200.00		$200.00
Gas	$45.00		$45.00
TOTAL			**$481.63**
Remaining Funds	*$318.37*		Monthly Total
Starbucks	$4 coffee	2x a week	$32.00
Manicure	$20 w/tip	1x a month	$20.00
Liquor Store	$12 wine/$8 liquor	1x a month	$20.00
EATING OUT			
Breakfast	$18	1x a week	$72.00
Lunch	$9	1x a week	$36.00
Dinner	$30	1x a week	$120.00
			$300.00
TOTAL			**$781.63**

TOPIC #26: THINKING ABOUT YOUR FUTURE

College is consistently branded as the "best four years of your life," and that may be true. However, I feel like there is a close battle between the 18-22 year-old life I'm just leaving and my 22-30 year-old future.

It is scary. There is no doubt about that. This is when mom and dad snip your wings and lightly push you out of the nest into the world of being a grown up. With great freedom comes great responsibility: getting a job, learning how to budget, absorbing your own expenses and truly be on your own for the first time. This is a period of great change but it is also a time of great excitement and potential. You are on the cusp of the greatest time of your life; however, it is up to you how you approach it.

If you choose to stick your head in the sand and refuse to pay attention to your "grown up" responsibilities, life is going to be VERY tough.

You may not want to admit this, but you are leaving the easiest years of your life. Sure, getting up and going to your chemistry lab after a long night of Thirsty Thursday could be considered "hard," but that is not "real world hard" – that was "college hard." Working 8:00 AM-5:00 PM makes college look like a cakewalk. You will be far ahead of your peers if you choose to focus on your future now and make good decisions that will benefit you down the road.

When students graduate college, some immediately need to go into the workforce. They do not have a stable family behind them who can financially provide for them any longer. Others take some time off to travel or "find themselves." Whether you are sitting in a cubicle or traveling the South of France, "finding yourself" is something we ALL need to do.

You have one person you can *always* rely on in creating your future, and that is you! Family is going to be there to support you along your way, but they cannot create your life for you. It is something that comes with growing up. Don't complain when life gets tough. Put on your "big girl panties" and DEAL with it in an appropriate manner. Life is 20% of what happens to you and 80% of how you react to it.

TOPIC #27: GETTING A JOB

Ready or not...time to get a job!

RÉSUMÉ

The first step to landing a job is having more than your stellar personality...you need a little piece of paper to back up how awesome you are. This is known as your *résumé*. A lot of times you will have other things helping you get in the door (connections are SO important – we'll discuss that later), but that is not always the case.

Sometimes your application is a shot in the dark and the only thing the employer will have to get to know you is by this piece of paper with your name, work experience and accomplishments. It is vital to make this a shining portrayal.

Here are the things you should include on your résumé. There are numerous online sources that can provide you with examples.

- Contact Information (full name, email, address)
- Education (college, field of study, GPA, graduation date)
- Relevant Work Experience (internships, summer jobs)
- Volunteer Experience (throughout college)
- Relevant Skills
- References

There are some noteworthy dos and don'ts when crafting your résumé.

Beginning with your contact information, make sure it is accurate and up-to-date. Also, you want to present yourself as professionally as possible. Do not put your AIM email account from high school of blondebabe94@aol.com. You possibly will need to create a new professional email account if you do not have one. Another recommendation would be to not use your college email. Some schools restrict access to these accounts post graduation and you don't want people unable to contact you. Have a simple account name such as your first and last name and make sure to check it frequently.

After you give the details of your college education (leave high school behind!), you should list your work experience with your most recent mentioned first. Some résumé examples suggest that you only include relative work experience, but you should tailor your resume to each place you apply, as they most likely will be looking for different skill sets. It is important to provide a brief description of your tasks you have performed at each place of employment. This is your opportunity to customize your life story to the job you are hoping to get.

When I worked as an intern at a boutique I was asked to do things like flipping through catalogues to discover new trends and what was going to be in style in the next season. However, when I was applying for an investment banking internship, the experience of knowing boyfriend jeans were coming back into style would not have been a good selling point.

Instead of putting "browsed catalogues" on my résumé, I said the store manager taught me how to calculate optimum pricing of products because that was more relevant to the job I was trying to obtain. NEVER fabricate tasks, work experience – or anything else – to try to look more impressive. Simply use common sense when choosing what description to add.

When listing honors and activities, they should come from college. After you finish high school, you should leave that in the past. If you are a senior in college it really isn't relevant that you were in the band when you were a freshman in high school. However, if you graduated high school as the class Valedictorian that would be a good thing to leave in. Once again, use common sense.

High school college counselors push the importance of volunteer experience, and it is still relevant when trying to get a job today. Employers want to see that you are involved and invested in more than just bettering yourself. Many workplaces also have community service days, so an expectation of volunteerism is still is an integral part of your paying job. Make sure you are giving back not only for your résumé, but because it is the right thing to do and can help you grow in many ways.

Relevant skills will be tailored, once again, to the job in which you are applying. These could include things such as accounting if you minored in something like this in college. If you are very proficient at things such as Microsoft Excel and PowerPoint, then include.

References are also a very important aspect to your résumé. These should be people that can attest for your character and skills. Many times these people will be former employers who have offered to help you obtain future jobs. These individuals don't have to be people you have worked with but could be close family friends.

When asking someone to be on your résumé make sure they will vouch for you and know you well enough to answer questions a potential employer may ask them. Keep these references updated on future jobs in which you are applying and when employers potentially may be calling them.

It is a bad idea to have someone on your résumé and then not update he or she on your activity for two years and then are blindsided by a reference call. All about maintaining good relationships!

INTERVIEWS

Once you have your foot in the door, interviews will make or break you. You could have a stellar résumé; 4.0, double major, lots of extracurricular activities, but if you can't hold a conversation with an interviewer you can pretty much kiss the opportunity goodbye.

All employers are looking for different traits in candidates. For some positions they are looking for outgoing individuals who can command a room (think of applying for a sales position). Others may be tailored to someone quieter who enjoys being behind the scenes (a software analyst).

Play on your strengths and know what an employer is looking for. Hopefully you know about the company and the position so you will know if it suits your personality or not.

DO YOUR RESEARCH

Don't ever come to an interview empty minded. Research, research, research! By that I mean make sure to do your due diligence on the company – research is the key. Interviewers are known for asking "do you have any questions for me?" Your response should not be "um yeah...so what exactly do you guys do here?" or "where is your office headquartered?" You should already know the answers to these questions. Don't simply ask questions to fill the silence.

A good question to ask would be "what is the corporate environment like with this company? Does it involve a lot of teamwork?" That is a good question. Or, "I know your headquarters are located in New York; which other offices compare to that office in size? Do young people tend to start at the large offices?"

Applicants can use Google in order to find out which questions an interviewer may ask. **Glassdoor.com** is a wonderful website where people actually report interview questions from different companies. You can search the company at which you are applying and will find reviews of average salaries, company reviews and interview questions from the company's current or former employees.

Do NOT rely solely on these questions. You should ask yourself the hard questions you might encounter, such as "explain to me a time when you had a problem and you didn't know how to solve it...what did you do?" That seems like a simple question but coming up with an answer that is intelligent and relevant is sometimes difficult to do on the spot (trust me: I butchered interviews when I was a sophomore).

Bottom line: be yourself. Present your most authentic self because that is who you want them to hire and that is who you will soon show them you are every day. Do not portray yourself other than you truly are because they will hire that person, not you. Don't walk in and have a conversation like you would have with one of your friends about getting wasted at the bar for A&M weekend.

Be professional, intelligent, classy and – most of all – confident. You'll wow them!

TOPIC #28: DRESS TO IMPRESS

Although I've been encouraging you to keep track of how you spend your "want" money and to curb your shopping...here is an exception.

Most of you probably do not have a wardrobe full of blazers and appropriately long dresses and skirts – not exactly bar attire. In order to put your best foot forward as you begin the trek toward adulthood you must dress the part. While looking the part is only half the battle, it is still very important.

Last spring a few students and I had a meeting with two women who have been working in our industry for quite some time. One of the women harped on the idea of knowing whom you are dressing for. She told the story of a girl who went to a client meeting with the CEO of a company. The man was in his 60s and came from humble beginnings. The young girl came in wearing a brand new pair of Christian Louboutins, and the CEO declined to put her on the account.

This story bugged me after I heard it. I enjoy nice things. I have nice clothes, bags, shoes, and jewelry, and it irked me to hear that the only reason this man didn't want to do business with this woman was because she came stomping into the meeting in $1,000 shoes (granted I do not know this girl and she could have been completely wrong for the account, but this was the only piece of the story that reached me).

The CEO disliked the fact that she felt entitled to come in at that age wearing shoes that were so expensive. Now, I still don't 100% agree with his decision, but I do think it provides a good lesson.

Most people you will be interviewing with will be older than you. They will have been in your chosen industry for quite some time and they have "paid their dues," and they'll expect those coming up behind them to do the same.

This leads to a different topic. Numerous studies have been done that people our age – those in Generation X – believe we are entitled to large positions and paychecks far before being of any value to a firm. We do not want to begin at the bottom.

Back to the Louboutin case. Possibly the shoes were a gift, possibly this was a purchase long she saved up for...you don't get the chance to explain that in a meeting! Someone's first impression of you may be completely skewed by what you are wearing or the accidental façade you are giving off. You only get ONE shot to make a first impression.

So when in doubt, don't wear it. When I first heard this story I wondered why I should change who I am and try and cover up the fact that I like nice things just to avoid putting someone off? That is not the point. You may love the finer things in life but someone else may not have those same means – or the same priorities – and may not respect someone who may seem to throw money around.

Bottom line: be yourself. But also think about "how" you're being you. "You" may be the girl who likes to wear super tight BCBG bandage skirts to the bars accompanied with 4 inch Jeffrey Campbell heels, but you wouldn't wear that to a lunch with your grandmother or to impress your new boss.

What you wear is the first thing someone notices when you walk in the door. When beginning my process of interviewing for internships, many guides and friends told me I needed to go buy a suit. A suit? Are you kidding me? Absolutely not. I would never wear that to an interview because that is NOT me. That would be putting on a false façade. Instead I wore a knee length tweed skirt with a chic white blouse.

Rule of thumb is always dress comfortably for an interview. Don't strut up in there in your college sweats and hair in a bun, but also do not go in and present yourself in a way that is uncomfortable for you. If the workplace only wants someone who does dress like that, chances are that "environment" is not for you.

Go in and wow them with more than your outfit, but use common sense. Keep it minimal and classy...in your OWN way. Never try to be someone else or you will end up unhappy with your job and your employer will be unhappy with you.

The best way to approach new work clothes is to look for things you can wear lots of ways. Look for a top that would go with a navy, white or brown pencil skirt or pants. Find a dress that can be layered with a blazer for the winter and a light cardigan for the summer. Look for versatile shoes, from flats of a neutral color (brown to nude) to black pumps that can be worn with every outfit.

Think savvy when buying your new wardrobe and you can eliminate having to fork out even more money in the future if your taste is too trendy.

According to the Center for Talent Innovation, women are "a growing market, exercising decision-making control of an estimated $11.2 **trillion** in investable assets" (Tara Siegel Bernard, "Financial Advice for Women, From Women," *New York Times*, 11/7/15, B1). Girls, in order to be the boss of THAT MUCH money...we sure want to be looking the part too!

TOPIC #29: NOT ALWAYS WHAT YOU KNOW

Connections are a great thing. Whether these are your parents' friends, esteemed alumni or simply connections you have made on your own, people help you get places. They can open new doors for you and broaden your horizons to consider opportunities you may be overlooking.

What type of person are you when you board an airplane? Are you the person who gets on, slides on your new Chanel sunglasses, turns up your iPod and then passes out for the duration of the flight? Or are you the person who immediately introduces yourself to your neighbor? You ask them where they're from...what their story is.

I ask this because these are situations where incredible things can occur. It is trite but true that things in life happen when you least expect them. A door can open when speaking to someone in the line at Starbucks. If you just stand there and don't attempt to engage with the person next to you, you will never know what that interaction could have been.

These interactions can be absolutely nothing but putting a smile on someone's face. Or that brief conversation could lead to getting a business card, which then gets you in with one of their friends who is the C.M.O. of a marketing company who is hiring for a position that is exactly what you have been looking for. Bottom line: you never know.

A big part of having good connections, and making new ones, is ensuring these are genuine connections. No one likes that person who only calls when they need something. If you really want to leave a lasting impression on someone, be that person who shoots them an email to check in and see how they are doing when you don't need anything.

Have no agenda behind your relationship. If you don't jive well with someone or get along with them, don't force a relationship just because it may get you places. Relationships like that usually don't end well and are very transparent.

Never count out an opportunity or where it could lead you down the road. Just because you have a connection that isn't able to direct you where you want to be right now doesn't mean that in the future your path can't change. People are amazing and the places a genuine connection can take you are infinite.

Approach every day with an open mind and your best foot forward because you never know who you're going to meet and how that can propel you to reaching your dreams.

A great tip I tell all my friends to look into is the alumni feature on LinkedIn (if you don't have a LinkedIn profile I strongly recommend getting one).

The alumni tool allows you to search graduates from your university that work in a variety of fields in numerous cities. Alumni are usually very willing to help young graduates reach their dreams in some form or fashion. The legwork is all on you, but don't feel afraid to reach out and ask for help.

TOPIC #30: OPPORTUNITY OVER MONEY

When choosing your first job, or at any point in your life, one thing you should not necessarily do is take the job that is offering you the most money. In some instances, money is an absolute need and you have to take that job to pay your bills. However, if your budget is at all flexible, weigh your options. Which option is going to give you the best opportunity? Which option is going to be able to open the most doors for you?

Let's say you have two job offers. One paying $50,000 and another paying $40,000. The $50,000 a year gig is great: it is with a Fortune 500 company (the top 500 companies are ranked by *Fortune* magazine each year) with good benefits, and would be a very safe bet. The $40,000 gig is also great, but in different ways. You entered into talks with this company because someone you really admire got you in the door.

If you take this opportunity you will be giving up $10,000 and possibly some benefits but what will you gain? You could gain the opportunity of working under someone you truly admire and can learn a lot from.

126

A recent article in the *Wall Street Journal* looked at how employees who feel upper management is tracking them usually perform better and show more of a work ethic than those who do not feel management is noticing them. Those who might not have tight connections with the **C-suite** (CEO, CFO, CMO – any top executive) may not feel like they are in a position to be promoted to bigger and better opportunities.

Although hard work should shine through, connections or not, choosing your job based on who you know is a reasonable thing to keep in mind. Going into a job where you have a few key connections and where you know people are looking out for you is comforting. This does not mean you can slide in and coast your way to an executive position, but that may provide a little more cushion than you would have had elsewhere.

There are numerous other things you will weigh when considering different career opportunities. At the end of the day, talk to your family and look at your budget, but in the end go with your gut. It usually doesn't steer you wrong.

IN CLOSING

"Money does not grow on trees." What a cliché, but OH SO true! This is going to become more and more apparent as you begin this new chapter of your life.

Life is all about decisions. Should I go to this college? Should I take this job? Should I go on a date this guy? Should I buy these shoes? What may seem like an innocent and small decision ultimately can lead to a huge learning lesson. If you buy those $300 shoes, you possibly have just spent half of your "want" money for the month. The bottom line is responsibility.

Being in control of your finances and realizing that you need to set a budget for yourself is both a humbling and an empowering experience. You may have gone through life not looking at price tags and felt it really didn't matter because "hey I'm young…why not buy it?!" Can you splurge every once in a while? Yes. Can you do it every day? No.

Hopefully this book has enlightened you a little bit about the tough reality of "reality." These segments are key things everyone needs to know, but as women, we may have fallen behind.

I truly believe each of you can change the world. Women are incredible beings and we have the advantage being young and having the whole world before us. Go out there and chase your dreams. If you aim high enough it is very unlikely you will fail completely.

Be thankful for yourself because you're all you have. Life's no rehearsal so do it well!

Shoot for the moon, land amongst the stars.